oblivion, tyrants, crumbs

To Judge Bernini,
with best wishes,

May 15, 2009

OBLIVION

TYRANTS

CRUMBS

❖

POEMS *by* JOHN LEVY

❖

FIRST INTENSITY PRESS
LAWRENCE, KANSAS

This book is for Leslie,
Nat, Ally, Zoe and Harrison

First Edition

Cover painting: Leslie Buchanan
Book design: Lee Chapman

First Intensity Press
P.O. Box 665
Lawrence, Kansas 66044
email: leechapman@aol.com
www.FirstIntensity.com

I am grateful to the editors who originally published some of these poems, sometimes in earlier versions, in the following magazines: *CLWN WR; Cue: A Journal for Prose Poetry; First Intensity; Flute; House Organ; Legal Studies Forum; Longhouse; Madrona; Messages from the Heart; Minotaur; Noon: journal of the short poem; Plucked Chicken; Poetry Salzburg Review; Shearsman; Shuttle; Text; The Southeastern Review*; and *Workshop*.

I thank Bob Arnold of Longhouse, the late Ed Cain of tencrow press, R. J. Ellis of Sow's Ear Press, John Martone of tel-let, David Miller of Kater Murr's Press, and Tom Raworth of Infolio, for publishing some of these poems, occasionally in variant forms, in broadsides and chapbooks. In 2003 John Martone published a chapbook with the same title as this book and I especially want to thank him for publishing four chapbooks of my poetry; his interest and care have been crucial. Also, the late James L. Weil, of The Elizabeth Press, published some of these poems in a 1980 book, *Among the Consonants*, and I am fortunate to be one of the poets he counseled and befriended.

I am grateful to Rupert Loydell and David Miller who included a few of these poems in two anthologies they edited: *How the Net is Gripped: a selection of contemporary American poetry* (Stride, 1992, Devon, England) and *A Curious Architecture: a selection of contemporary prose poems* (Stride, 1996).

Philip Rowland and I have been writing collaborative poetry, in which we respond to each other's poems, for several years. Some of the poems in this book are directly inspired by his poems.

Many friends have helped me over the years. I gratefully acknowledge Alex Anderson, Bob Arnold, Guy Birchard, Lee Chapman, the late Cid Corman, James Elkins, Tony Frazer, Cralan Kelder, Alan Chong Lau, the late Robert Lax, John Martone, Brian Metcalf, David Miller, J.K. Osborne, the late Carl Rakosi, Boyer Rickel, Philip Rowland, Arthur Statman, Paul Watsky, the late James L. Weil, and Vassilis Zambaras for providing friendship, invaluable help, and support.

My interest in poetry was sparked by my older brother Ed's love of poetry and I gladly recognize my debt to him. My parents have been wonderfully encouraging and generous and I dedicate this book to them. I also dedicate this book to my wife, Leslie Buchanan, and my two children, Nat and Ally, for their encouragement, patience, understanding, and for the countless ways they have influenced and inspired me.

—JL

— CONTENTS —

atmostair

vermilion grass and bluest word

white pages blackened

the whole shit and caboodle

receiver

sporadic-E phenomenon

this blotesque self

out of the land of minus

released

light, mind, mood, shade

dogs named Bingo

question marks, stars, arrows

inside its sound

bones and dreams

ATMOSTAIR

DEALT

The rat of spaces. The ace of lies. The ten of
horror. Deuce of stone. The jack is dressed

in a potato costume, you can see his dark eyes:
the jack of insanity. The queen of

addictions is almost nude, her bikini top
old, discolored. The king of lies (there are two cards

for liars) is shown in a small room
surrounded by corpses. The bumpkeeper

is the dealer, never cheats
in any way you can detect. You stare,

rarely with disbelief, at each card.
The nine of despair, six of lust,

four of betrayal, three of shame. Five of
helplessness. The seven of bitterness and resentment

is a cluttered collage, small
dark scenes, ugliness. Sometimes

you manage to discard. Sometimes
you feel free.

Brambles scribble, bamboo does not, roses address. Leaves, together in breezes, in branches. A day with so much sound and all of it song. Birds in trees. Bees in tall asphodels. The Greek boy studying English makes up a word: atmostair. A Greek girl writes of her family holiday: "Failures were forgotten and we looked on the bright of things." Robert Lax says: "think the thing to try to be in the body of the universe is one good microbe."

CNN (Sept. 2005)

During a report about Hurricane Katrina, the well-
dressed man talking was smooth enough until
he got to a sentence that was ordinary enough and

paused, unexpectedly, then said the word
"morgue," but said it slower
than anything else he'd said. Said it

as if the word came to life

and death

for him, in the middle of the
routine of talking into a lens. He isolated
the word, as if surprised it had

come out of him and unsure
he could recover

and gab away again. He said it
so slowly it sounded, first, like more

before the gh came

or did it sound like maw

then rg –

I'm not sure and he, too,
seemed to need to think and feel before he could get it

out.

Paper Wasp (12/2/06, Tucson)

"Wasps
don't have eyelids. Their eyes
stay open after they're dead."

I say this aloud. Ally, 9, says "Yuck!"
Its black eyes huge on the small head. She leans over and
stares. I found it on its back, near her, as she knelt

in our yard looking for sand rubies. As I study it she moves
to our small slide, though doesn't
go down it. "I prefer not

looking at dead things," she says from
where she stands above me. I ask her to come back
and look again, telling her I'd love to hear her describe it

because I know she'll say things
I wouldn't think of. Without moving
from where she stands atop the slide's

metal ladder, she says, "Its black eyes
lost their twinkle
and gained

a musky look."

Change Each Time

as a child I hoped for
skywriting
but was pleased by the solitary
lines
that whitely, slowly, came apart

* * *

She asked me if she should say
"in a manner of seconds" or "in a matter of seconds" –

unable to remember which

is the cliche

and wanting to use
the cliche.

* * *

Twilight
through telephone wires, a musical staff
with no notes
but color.

* * *

WATCH THE WORLD ARGUE, ARGUE WITH ITSELF.
Black ink on an oak table in the law school library.

Above it, in blue ink, in equally blocky letters: PISS OFF.

Under both of them, in small, neatly penciled rounded script:
Who's going to teach me peace and happiness?

18

*　*　*

a solution, in music

solution, from Latin solvere,
to loosen, unfasten, untie,
solve, dissolve

the solution in music

the time

in music

like a dream of sound, one
we can choose

whenever we want

once we know where it is

though the it
and is

change each time

*　*　*

almond blossoms
in grey dusk appear
as if their tree weren't there

*　*　*

At six I polished Lincoln
with my pencil eraser until he'd glow
on every penny.

I'd say, but never aloud
if anyone could hear,
"Four score

and seven
years ago our
fathers. . ." Those words,

over and over, with long,
sweet
pauses.

                    *   *   *

"My grandfather," I overhear my eleven-
year-old say to his pal at the park, "was on a
destroyer
that got hit by a kamikaze." He says it
with pride. I hadn't realized he cared.

Paul Klee, Drafted at 35

for David Miller

World War I, a red piece of paper from the German government: Klee must enter the infantry. Issued a helmet removed from a corpse. Transfers to flying school, varnishes wings.

Transfers to another flying school, works in the paymaster's office, finally has a place where he can close a door and be alone. His office near the landing strip.

Planes have canvas skin. After the planes crash and the dead are pried out, and/or washed out, Klee walks over to the mess to cut off pieces of unburnt canvas. He paints in a desk drawer he shuts when he hears footsteps.

Paul Klee

Klee close to death
drawing angel after

angel

a man and his angels

angels and their man

GOAT OUTSIDE A GREEK VILLAGE

Bright day out on the low hill with no
other human around, a penned-in goat and I
began a longish talk in Goatish. I don't know

any other time I've put more
emotion into what I've said. We each
waited for the other's

silence
before we began again our songlike replies
and wails. Goatese. It did ease

something in me, something
I could never translate, but shared
that long once. I began the talk

because I loved a poem
by Umberto Saba about talking
to a bleating goat.

I hadn't imagined how much it would hurt
to walk away, finally, the goat
crying out, waiting, trying yet again

Between Cages at the Zoo

3-year-old girl, alone,
stands on, and bends
over, the grated rain gutter

looks down into it

sticks
her fingers through

and shouts
into the darkness
Hi

VERMILION GRASS AND BLUEST WORD

LEMON RED

for Cralan Kelder

Lemon Red is the title of one of your
poems and one of your books.

Orange caw, white crow. Vermilion grass
and bluest word. Light poem

and deep Kelder. The white eloquence
of stars and black eloquence of night.

Invent a name for yourself
like finding that lemon red, finding the

last stop the poem makes then getting
back on it

and taking the journey again. Round
trip, lemon's

shape, Eureka –

Eureka lemon, most widely grown
variety. Take any lemon,

let your hand cup it, feel
how it pulls down your arm

somewhat like it weighed
the branch. The point of a poem is rarely like

the lemon's point, the whole tapering
to a rounded stop.

amount of sense (Pound, Spicer). Or the
opposite – like Bunting. Levy? An amount
taxed? Troops mustered? Except

my family pronounces it to rhyme with
TV, not bevy, so that puts Levy into the enormous
Meaningless Name School of Poets, with

Niedecker a nearby neighbor on
one side and Kenward
Elmslie going the other way though he

has the distinction of argu-
ably
having a meaningless first

and last as if he himself were hurtling syllables
"thanks to a blessed motor disturbance in the Heavens"

VAST ORANGE

Vast orange liberties stir within the poem.

That's not
what Ted Berrigan wrote.

In his sonnet he mentions, first,

"A vast orange library of dreams"

and a few lines later

"Vast orange libraries of dreams
Stir inside 'The Poems.'"

In Berrigan's
poems

orange occurs
with an orange frequency.

Naked, Short Poems

According to Alice Notley, "A short poem
is peculiarly naked. . ."

Ah, peculiar
nakedness

keeps

your attention

a bit
longer.

The shorter the poem the more
peculiar

its
body

parts.

A long poem
dressed for winter

as the short one stripped
to skinny-

dip in the white
page

Poem

We are the authors of this animal,
the creators of its setting.

The page a white sea.

Our home
with its great view of the sea.

Any time
we have

for poems

is a time
we have good luck.

A time we have
to listen to.

We are the time of this good luck,
we are it breathing.

My Library

It's no fortress.

But that word tress in there
has something of the loveliness

of my books, of being surrounded
by books.

When I'm dead
no one will love them

as I have. I even love to hold them
when they're closed.

I chose them
to keep. They keep me

like an anti-cage. They
open me and provide

a good deal
of my paroles.

Orgasm, Penciled In

The more I buy used poetry books
the more I find penciled remarks
and the more I think the handwriting that seems feminine

yields the interesting. Or maybe it's the men,
too, whose writing looks feminine
whose responses are more curious. Up

near the title of one poem is written,
very small, orgasm, symmetry
with that comma spaced between the words like this:

orgasm   ,   symmetry

–Disappointingly, at least to me, when I
look closely at the tiny cursive it's
oronym – a word I don't know

that turns out not to appear
in my big dictionary. So turn to the Oxford
English Dictionary, keeper of the obsolete, to find

no oronym either. Dear unknown reader,
holding your sharpened pencil, I'm sure
you had no idea you'd give me

false hope with your minuscule
cursive, your promising, promiscuous
Latin. Nym, numb, nymph, word

play, your penciled comment above the poem
like foreplay, denumbing and happily disturbing,
longhand, longing, your gift of a mirage.

Surrealist Anthology

Some of the best poems anyone ever wrote
have been put into this thick book then sunk.

In your antique diver's suit, like a big lunk, you
go down into the dark

to find this loot. The unglued pages
float in wide circles around the book's

gently flapping wings. Tristan Tzara speaks
of the rain of stone teeth while nearby Breton

says his wife's arms
are of sea foam.

Two Poems

Looks like just one, though, doesn't it?

Go ahead, split it with an axe
like the first one you saw as a child

or the first one you ever lifted and swung
into wood. Swing your wood-

handled axe through the unhandled
air, here, handle it. Make it split. Give

yourself the

pleasure of
being

an editor, an un-
surpassed

un-
impassed

little journey through some
one else's

little journey.

An editor, an axitor, an aviator, a
maze subscriber, O scribe here

you could even cut that O
in half. Timber!

THE RUSTY POEM

for Philip Rowland

The rusty poem doesn't have to arrive.
In fact, it didn't.

Yang Lian writes: "the rusty train doesn't have to arrive"

Philip Rowland is trying to develop
Yang Lian's line

into a poem, "though it hasn't quite arrived yet."

I'm waiting at the village train station, looking down the
long line of track one way, the other way, then back.

Nothing is arriving, surrounded by the scenery.

It's great to be here, at the station, nothing

else to do except
wait for something that simply

won't arrive
simply. I do an about-face

to watch it
as it doesn't arrive that way either.

(after Basho)

My poems aren't
really mine. Any more

than a frog
owns its croak

or its splash as it dives
beneath the green surface.

You see the surface translated
into language

ripples. (The frog invisible,
immersed.)

WHITE PAGES BLACKENED

lightning scrapes night's paint to salt

AUTUMNAL PILGRIMAGES

for Zoe Levy

Millions
stepping out
(as they do

in Kyoto)
to pay homage to
each of the local

most celebrated
trees, trees famous

for bold reach of
branch or

deep wine-reds mixed
with gold, or just
for the bark, a

sycamore's grey
smooth bark

which has scaled to
reveal buff
or orange

BEACH AND TIME

for Robert Lax on Patmos

blue waves blue
waves blue as night
comes

darkening waves the
different
silence

as
night comes
darkening waves

night waves dark
then dark
then dark

VIEW

the blue waves
tell the truth
in the light

and at night they stretch it

TEMPLE GROUNDS IN KYOTO

the reflection of the tree
in the temple pond

a tall tree
a pond

a tree
a wide pond

a leafy tree
a pond

a tree
a still pond

a tree at the edge
of the pond

reflected
in the pond

the temple grounds

no one in sight
including yourself

ON THE GROUND

flock of
shadows
on the ground
(where else?)

      * * *

in my dirt driveway, mid-March, mid-
desert, a large rattlesnake mates
with the smaller one underneath – he
strokes his black forked tongue
across the top of her flat head
as I watch from above in an idling van

      * * *

guest stars
appear

to smal-
ler guests

looking
up

TUCSON, FOUR DAYS

after Halloween the two pumpkins up
on the tall white wall de-

compose, softening, co-

llapsing, open-

mouthed, folding
in

on themselves, their
empty carved out

smiles, wrinkled

as if in the last stages
in a nursing home. Almost all the

other pumpkins in the neighborhood
thrown out, though there are

ceramic and
plastic ones, the immortals.

Two Birds and Tall Tree

Those two crows standing together
on a snowy branch as snow

falls in front of and
behind them wear

snowflakes
on their feathers. Snow

dots my hair, lands
on my beak, wordless

falls
like white pages blackened

by no caw or word or curse. Crow
brain and my mind, cold

as the forked white and black
branches of this tree.

THE WHOLE SHIT AND CABOODLE

SHIT AND CABOODLE

My client said, "the whole shit and caboodle."
Was pleased when I told her
I'd write that down.

She has been going blind. In her forties, now,
in jail again, she is one of the cheerful ones.
She quit reporting to her probation officer after her man

beat her so bad she couldn't get out of bed
for weeks. "I left my purse behind
when I ran out of his place," she said.

"I didn't have the probation officer's phone number,
it was in my purse, and I was afraid
to go back." She began going blind

after a car accident 10 years ago, slow process
almost finished. What she said about her case:
"I want to solve

the whole shit and caboodle
problem." She told me to make sure to tell the judge
to release her from jail in daylight, because

she can still see a bit
and if she gets out at night
she won't stand a chance.

My Client

who committed his crime
drunk and then, still
drunk, confessed to the police
is angry

that he was indicted, keeps
telling me that someone else who did
something much worse
got off "scotch free."

The last thing he needs to
hear is
his vocabulary is also
in deep shit.

In the Eyes of the Hard

"In the eyes of the hard" is what
I read in her letter to the judge.

She was telling the sentencing judge all
about her life – and her letter,

single-spaced, hand-written, had words
jammed together. She wrote that she had always tried

to be good "in the eyes of the hard."
She's a heavy woman, plain, her

parents divorced, her own life
without lovers. All eyes are

hard, I thought, rereading her words.
That has been her life

and so she robbed someone to make her own life
a little better. I reread her words and saw

her h was supposed to be an L
though this capital L curves

in the middle of its bottom line,
as if that line has to cover a stone.

And what looks like an a is an o pushed
so close to the L and the r

it's hard to tell what it is. In the eyes of the
Lord, in the eyes of the hard, for her

there isn't much difference; she asks
for probation.

What's Dark and Whole?

Lies.

A liar may tell a falsehood, and nothing but
a falsehood, trying to gain a false-hold.

Yang Lian writes:
"no darkness has ever been a fragment" –

you can see what he means, images of dark
multiply and join, expanding. The darkness is not only

a thorn in the side, the darkness
is the thorn and the side and the entire

body and the whole plant the thorn grew out of
and why the body was near that plant

and why that plant needed to evolve
into a thorned form of life. Maybe nothing, dark or

light, is ever a fragment. No joke, no sob,
no orgasm, no dream, no starlight, no electron,

no birth, no word written in neon, no piece
of music. A man in chains

tells his lawyer his wife will write the judge on his behalf
and the wife, in the lobby outside the courtroom,

tells the lawyer her husband has lied so often
for the last twenty-one years

that she doesn't know what she could
say, in a letter, that will help him now.

He dropped out in third grade. I ask how many brothers and sisters he had. Alive? (He already told me some have died.) No, from the beginning. Six brothers, two sisters. I'm the baby. I never knew my father. I ask him to name his brothers. He names five. I say it sounds like he has five brothers. He says he has six, names them again, naming himself among them. I say he is counting himself as one of his brothers and he agrees. I say I have two brothers and so if someone asked how many brothers I have I'd say two. Oh, he says, I have five then.

This is the first time we've had a chance to talk. He's my client now (he was another lawyer's client when he was sentenced) because he violated probation. We talk about why he failed. He smoked crack and weed and got caught. His p.o. got drug counseling and mental health counseling for him and that helped. He stayed clean three months, then got caught drunk a few weeks ago. I ask why he was drinking. He says everyone in his family is dying and their funerals are in another state and he can't go to the funerals because the p.o. won't let him. He mentions all the deaths. There are so many I get lost. I ask him to list the deaths.

For six years in a row he has lost someone, beginning with his mother in oh two. A brother in oh three, another brother in oh four, an aunt in oh five, another brother in oh 6. He is 46, was in prison until oh four, then moved here to get away from the crackheads he was hanging out with. He hurt someone here in a fight so ended up on probation here. He says last year he was watching TV and someone described depression and it sounded like what he felt so he talked to his p.o. and the p.o. got him counseling and medication. He says the medication helps him a lot, but he can't remember its name. He was doing okay but then the p.o. caught him drinking. Why did you drink? Because my uncle died. He says this uncle had raised him, like a father, and died last month. He didn't tell anyone. I ask why he didn't tell his p.o., to explain why he was drinking. He says it hurts too much to talk and what good would it do, the p.o. wouldn't have let him go to the funeral.

He wants another chance on probation. I say I'll help him write a letter to the judge. I suggest he tell the judge about the deaths in his family so the judge will understand his situation. He agrees. I ask if he knows the word grief. He says he has never heard of it. I try to explain it and he says he gets it. I tell him about grief counseling and he says maybe that would help. He dictates to me what he wants to say to the judge and I print, trying to form my letters well (the way I did in fourth grade) so that the judge (a judge who sometimes comments on defendants' penmanship) will like my printing. A double-spaced, handwritten letter, five pages long. I ask if he can sign his name. He signs in cursive and his signature is lovely.

Tooth Fairy, Esq.

My two children, son 11 and daughter 8, know
either I or their mother sneaks money
under their pillows. They know I'm sometimes
their tooth fairy. But what of

my client who told the social worker who
interviewed him in jail – when she asked
about his relationship to me, his public defender, that
"He's like the tooth fairy." When she asked him why, he said,

"He's the one who'd put money under the pillow."
It wasn't his only odd answer. When he boasted
he knows about biographies and was asked to explain, he said,
 "Biographies is a person's body movement. Autobiography

is how a person thinks." He, like me, is a father.
When asked about his children, he answered,
"I may make childish decisions." Asked
what he likes to eat, he said, "I eat my thinking." I, somewhat
    ashamed,

admit to a sweet tooth for oddness, admit loving the idea
that instead of being his lawyer I grew wings, became a
gentle presence who doesn't disturb a dream
and whose every visit enriches.

RECEIVER

I'm Writing a Poem about Death

Quote Louis Zukofsky's line about when
"we will lie as faceless as the grass"

then write about being a pallbearer
at my uncle's funeral six days ago.

Allyson, four-and-a-half, comes into the kitchen,
drags a wooden chair next to me, stands on it and looks

into my ear. She says, "You're only
a skeleton

with a costume on."

HEAVEN

First they take your phone numbers. The ones
you never forgot. Your home
when you were ten, your home
when you died, your best friends,
9-1-1, and all the others. They are going to use
that room in your memory, your

soul, for something new now, something
that has nothing to do
with numbers, but much
to do with love, that part in you
without limit, which is one of the reasons
you reached Heaven.

Ed Cain (1935 - 2001)

(1)

As a painter you loved
many colors, including
black. Eight months ago
you shot yourself. If these nine lines
were black bands
they'd wrap my fingertips
up to my shoulder.
As if I'd dipped my arm
into your death.

(2)

I'm on a bus going home. I'm writing
yet another poem to you because
I don't want your death. Hear that,
Ed? This is the one thing you gave me
that I don't want.

(3)

Strange to say, of a
suicide, he died
"by his own hand."
Yes, I get it, but
I insist now
that it is
stranger to say
that
than to say he
killed himself. Don't
ask me why. I think
of you, Ed, I think
of you often. Yes, you
used your hand to
pull the trigger.
The one you painted with.
Your own hand, the one
you stared at as a child
looking at the lines on your palm.
Dead by his own hand.
Dead by his own hand.
Dead by his own hand.
Tell me that isn't strange.
Repeat it and tell me, Ed,
it isn't awful.
Tell me, Ed, why you
couldn't wait for
God's hand, or for blind dumb deaf
fate, or for your own faulty heart.
Tell me why you couldn't wait
for whatever you believed you believed
was too fucking slow.

(4)

After I've thought of my friend, after
I've written poems to him, looked
at his paintings, loved
what he was able to do
and hated what he finally did,
I hear some bird outside and
think of him, who loved birds
and music and color and so much
and yet pulled a trigger. A trigger. Despair
not the word for it,
death self

imposed, death invited home,
move a finger and be no more,
be no, being gone. Leaving
us with these things you made
that don't die, where colors and forms
you worked to get right stay right:
this is who you are, this won't become was.

You can't take this away.

Do You

Do you have
to believe
in the (or
an) afterlife
to talk to the dead?

Because
I do. And don't.

ED CAIN'S SUICIDE

You're not here.

You're not here to tell me
which word you'd pick

for what it meant

to pull the trigger.

A friend told me you wouldn't agree
you decided to *destroy* your life. My friend

is right. So you choose.

You decided to quit trying?
You decided to allow yourself total control?
You decided to give up? Withdraw? Be released?
What?

You lifted everything you ever had, every
memory, every possibility, and
slammed the receiver down.

I'm still in the passenger seat the
last time you drove me to Sea-Tac airport.
Your old white van. We get in the short
line for the ferry, have
plenty of time (the ticket booth is closed). We're

the only ones to get out, go over
and look down at the water, see the gull
walk among the grit and rocks. Morning light.

ANOTHER FOR ED CAIN

If you were still
alive I'd

call you now and could

hear your voice, Ed,
hear you

talking
from the little house you

built
yourself

in the woods.
Listen to you tell me what is going on

in your life, but it was a life you
decided to destroy

so I'm talking to your silence
you shot here.

An afterlife? Suns explode yet souls cohere? The hereself
shall become the voyeur thereself? A soul
outlasts a body, views the living die forever?
Cavemen spirits watched the Thingmount, the
Parliament, Saddam hang and Bush chatter?

The Grim Reaper

Sure he's grim, but last time he came by I stalled him
by complimenting him on his posture.

With a shy smile he said he had to credit
his mother – she had taught him to stand tall.

Somehow we got onto grammar. He lamented
that a double negative

cancels out the negativity instead of making it
twice as powerful. Then he told his favorite joke, the one

about how some literary critics are grim
readers. Smiling a last time, he said he'd

"depart for now," adding that he loves
the word "depart."

HEARSE

It hears nothing. It is no
enormous ear on wheels, nor begins

pronounced like hear. A hearse, in twelve-
ninety-one, was a "flat framework for candles, hung

over a coffin." That was in Anglo-Saxon. Before that, in
Latin, it meant "harrow." Further back, in Oscan,

hearse comes from "wolf," the allusion
supposedly is to a wolf's teeth. Here,

in English, what is hear doing there? There is
nothing to hear

from the boxed corpse. It could be a stone
cushioned in a coffin. There's death – and everything else

breathing around it. We hire the special car, with our
procession behind it, to drive one of our own to never again.

ALLYSON'S FURTHER THOUGHTS

Allyson, 8, leans against the
metal pole of the swing set
in our backyard, closes

her eyes. She says,
"Death
will be

like this, like
eyes closed, except
without a body."

SPORADIC-E PHENOMENON

6 on the Bus

(1)

I sit in front of a man about 55,
around my age. I begin to read.
"Forgive me, Lord," he whispers to himself.
I can't read now. He stops talking.

(2)

Woman, maybe 45, who must've slept out all night
sits at 6 a.m. on the bus bench wrapped in a very small
white blanket. Bus arrives, she and I get on, and she rides

only about two miles, exits into a middle-class
residential neighborhood.

(3)

At the jail bus stop, I get on with a smiling gap-toothed
young man who goes and sits next to an older sullen man
at the back of the bus. The young guy
loudly brags he has been in jail

four times now!

"Same here," the older man says happily,
suddenly jaunty.

(4)

"He fell over," the woman on the bus
says to her children as we leave the downtown
bus station and we all look out
at the grey-haired thin man being lifted now by two
young men dressed as thugs. They
steady the old man upright
next to his metal walker
as we drive away.

(5)

And now, riding home on the bus, beginning of
dusk. All reds call out to me: the red
tail-lights, bank sign, the red cars and trucks,
then the stop sign and again all those brake lights
almost all the same shade of bright red, different
shapes and heights and for this moment
they fill the frame of the bus's wide windshield.

(6)

Shockingly happy middle-aged African-American woman
in scorching summer Tucson heat is lifted
onto the bus by the elevating ramp and wins over
the tough crowd on this jammed bus by nimbly
spinning her wheelchair around and executing a perfect
reverse drive to where she'll be secured into place while
there are cheers from her admiring fellow passengers.
This
is
a performance!

ALL OF US REGULARS ON THE EXPRESS

Woman two seats up
knits, black material. Mentally disturbed
man across from me for years has whistled,
hissed, guffawed, rarely speaks
words, loudly makes sounds a toddler
might make pretending to be a train or
rocket, bus or snake, plus he jitters
his hand in the air in what seems frantic
private sign language. He must weigh over 300 pounds, wears
blue jeans too tight, is about 30. We're regulars.
A friend I made on this bus, years ago, sits

either in front of me or in back of me.
We're both named John. John reads
"A Review of the Sporadic-E Phenomenon"
in his magazine. Poetic theory? No. He just told me
his magazine is called World Radio. We pass
The Loft, a movie theater playing "The Puffy Chair." Haven't
heard of it. I imagine the chair a light
pastel color. Our seats are plastic, we sit on a small piece of
fabric over a thin pad. Little comfort. Bald man
who just got on licks his hand
and rubs a few strands across baldness. My fellow

regulars, looking lost, looking absorbed, looking
out the window, looking down, looking weary, we are no
peas in a pod, no band of brothers and sisters, though
we shake and vibrate as one
sporadically occurring isolated group of
lives. With the exception of the mentally ill man, when
we spot each other somewhere else – downtown, or in a
mall, we wave happily

as if to a good
friend, as if all
our time together
matters.

Public Transport, Morning Bus

A woman reads a paperback novel.
I wish
I'd written her book. She's

in her 20s, moving her lips.
It's seven twelve a.m. If she were reading my
book of poems, which

would I want her to read?
I don't know. She wears
no lipstick, the only garish thing about her

is the novel's bright cover and now
she closes the book and
her mouth, frowns. It seems

she didn't want to leave those words.
She doesn't know that, as she read, a man
in his 50s back here

made her the plot and
single page
of his attention.

Waiting for the Bus in Mid-September

About 6 a.m., on Broadway
in Tucson, dawn was
15 minutes ago and the sky

still deep with it. Across the six
lanes of black about 70 pigeons
suddenly rise off the gas station roof

to circle in wider and wider tight arcs
as if the roof were the bottom of a cup
and they rose to trace the cup's rim, all

close to each other as they swing
a sharply tilting circle around and around until
two break off in wobbling flight north

and after more spins three fly west as the rest keep
wheeling in the air until they all
drop

to the big flat roof, stand
along its edge. The young Hispanic man, thin
moustache, dressed for manual labor, who had commented

before they lifted off
that the bus is late, now says, "Makes you
tired

just looking at 'em." "Not me,"
I don't say, not wanting to seem delighted
by birds or happy to be awake and going

to earn bread. "Yeah," I say, almost dismissively,
"but that was beautiful." I add, "They got their
morning work-out." He gives me a laugh.

READING ON A BUS PASSING THE HOSPITAL

For a moment, after reading poetry criticism, couldn't remember
if the cemetery comes before or after the hospital
when driving east. Usually I don't feel this lost. An isolated piece of

rainbow
is like a faint tattoo across one dark grey cloud and a helicopter is
about to land on the hospital roof. I'd been surprised to read, just

before I looked up, this observation: "Silliman's poetry
is profoundly superficial. . ." Now the bus picks up speed
towards the cemetery where I attended the funeral of

a woman named Kettlewell. Her family handed out a collection of
her favorite jokes. I don't imagine I'll ever
go to another funeral where something like that

is distributed, people leafing through it
before the service began. It was a delight
learning about her life. I lost my place, though, right now,

can't find, in the article I was reading about Silliman, that part
I just quoted. Did I dream it? But now I think about pro-
found and pro-lost, the family as protectors, finders and

keepers, for whom little is superficial, really, if (and this
is one of those giant ifs) if the family does want
to keep finding rather than losing.

THIS BLOTESQUE SELF

Rorschach

My life as a hut, a roar
shack, no

joke, all joke, ink
blot, ink botch, take a guess, live

a guess, look at this mess, an
ink

spill. My life an inked
shape on a page, a writer, an eraser, here

is my drafty shack, my hovel, I have
at it, tilt at it, go full tilt, half-tilt, full blot,

blottingly. And with this blotty paw
hand you this blotesque self

poured
onto, into, through a page.

CHILDHOOD SOLITUDE

I could count on
being by myself
when I took a bath. I
must've been five or

so. I'd tell myself the
stories I knew
endlessly because they wouldn't
end they'd

join each other. I'd be the
man who killed seven with
one blow and a little earlier the boy
who'd said the Emperor

had no clothes. I'd be up in the
crow's nest, up a bean stalk, inside a whale then
find myself wondering once again what
Grandpa meant when he asked,

What's black and white and red all over?

I told him I didn't know. He said,
A newspaper. And so there, alone, in the
bathroom, once again I'd think about how the grown-ups
hid almost everything from me. Newspapers

all about murders, so many photos with
so much red blood on every page that each page seemed
red all over. Where did they hide these newspapers?
Why tell me about them and expect me to laugh?

FROM CHILDHOOD

Dad would
show me
again

how to hold
a fork
as I cut meat

saying
I should be
able

to do this
perfectly

so I could eat
with royalty
and ship captains

in the afternoons
walking home
under the big trees

I'd look out
over the lake

the whole dining room
full of important people

and I was sitting
across from the captain

and he was talking
to me, only
to me

WHEN YOU WERE A CHILD

When you were a child
did you ever see one of those shows

where someone is locked in a room
and the walls and ceiling and floor all begin

to move closer
so the hero will be crushed. I knew there'd be

such a room waiting in the near
future.

Progress Report

I recently defected from the me me me, found
more yous and strangers. My self-portait poem now contains

bits of mirror in which you, reader, see
small pieces of yourself inside my own

pale head, pail head, bucket from when
I was a child and carried a bright bucket,

empty, happily, out onto the beach. Oh those
waves of sound. A poem's

sounds are the sounds' momentary destiny
if you read aloud or somehow

hear it inside. You may, yourself, after
you finish something like this, supply your own

"huh?"

Hope I didn't take it away from you
by saying it first. If a sponge

painted a self-portrait would it be a collection of
open mouths? And when that same sponge

writes a poem? What would it choose
as a nom de plume? A nom de spume?

OUT OF THE LAND OF MINUS

Two Paintings by Degas

"The Racehorse, Amateur Jockeys" took more than 13 years to not complete. Is that the opposite of racing?

Early on, after he'd started it, he promised the singer (for whom he'd agreed to paint it) he'd have it done in 5 days.

Nine years later the singer demanded it and Degas asked him to wait a few more days because it wasn't finished. Where, if anywhere, is the meaningless race against time?

About six months later the singer told Degas to hand it over or get sued. Degas surrendered it. The painting: several horses, four jockeys, two spectators in the foreground, a line of spectators distant enough to be a solid band of varied color, a small puffing locomotive, and behind that a hill with a road leading to houses, sky.

Years later, apparently within a short time, Degas painted a riderless horse and a fallen jockey. The horse turns his head to us as he leaps over the fallen man. No race anywhere in sight. The landscape simple now: grass and sky. The grass sketchy in places. Done, it looks unfinished.

BUSTS OF DIEGO GIACOMETTI

Alberto Giacometti made busts of his
brother, over and over
compressing that face into a slice

pressured, touched, pushed all over.
Alberto and Diego's mother
once told Alberto, "You'd

never win a
beauty contest." Another time she
in-

formed him
he looked as if he'd come
from a land of dark fogs.

He probably didn't
reply, "Yes, I'm
your son." Alberto

made Diego look
like he comes, gouged,
out of the land of minus.

LOUISE BOURGEOIS AND HER FATHER

Her father called her a useless
mouth. Father's

vain, cheating mouth, mouth of pain, mouth

that kissed women other
than Louise's mother. Louise

feared him. Her

sculpture, Destruction of the Father, an
enormous

sickening mouth, nightmare thing for a

tongue, a bad dream you
could walk into

awake.

Hollowed Section of Log

There it is, varnished, vertical on a wooden pedestal
in the living room of the Fullerton home, up
to a standing man's knees. "If that

thing
is a piece of art," Mrs. Clature
said, "it should have a title."

"Well. . ." Mr. Fullerton replied. "Well
is its title?" Mrs. Clature interrupted. "Like good?
Or like a well for water?" "No. . .I was going to say,

Well, it doesn't have a title. It isn't even called
untitled." "Got a shimmery kind of
associative emptiness to it," Mr. Clature noted, "like a word all

by itself, without the rest of the
message." "What word?" Mrs. Clature
demanded. "Unconscious," Mr. Clature ventured.

"Oh, you're only saying that
because you were reading Lacan in
bed last night," Mrs. Clature muttered.

"Our son made this and
gave it to us on our twenty-fifth
anniversary," Mrs. Fullerton said quietly.

THE WHITE TABLECLOTH

for James L. Weil

The orange rests
beside the blue plate.

The orange waits
beside the blue plate.

The orange has been
placed, bestowing

on the plate's rim
an edge of orange.

Beside it, not resting
or waiting, a peach.

Color Poem for Cralan Kelder

Glass green: a light
yellow green,
greener, lighter, stronger
than reed green and yellower and paler

than sky green. Glaucous: a pale yellow green or
light bluish grey
or bluish white

or a pale yellow,
yellower and stronger than smoke grey,
greener and deeper
than oyster grey

and yellower
than average Nile.

Something of a palette and something
of a vocabulary and something very partial
from the thin oval of the palette, with its

facticity and opening
for our thumb. The colors could blend but right here
are as lineated as a Josef Albers

on Cralan Kelder's wall in Amsterdam
where his infant daughter looks up in wonder.

MORANDI

More
and
I.

And,
and,
and.

More con-
tainers
and me.

Line
containers
up

to make a
sentence
that is is-

o-
lated
in a

quiet
room
where more

is and I
am
ajar.

POEM FOR LEE CHAPMAN ABOUT A COPY
SHE MADE OF AN EDWARD HOPPER DRAWING

Curtain
blowing

at the window
loneliness

inside and out

sole figure
maybe
figuring
out

in the wind

some thought

alone
with the wind

One-room studio apartment, thin walls. My neighbors' music off now. I walk to the bookshelf to look up a tree that grows at home, the jacaranda, but look instead at a postcard leaning against my books – an Egyptian sculpture. Seeing her, I take a handful of postcards from a stack. I'm looking for women. I pass Matisse, Vermeer . . . Choose Degas tonight.

A maid, standing behind a young woman, combing the woman's red hair. The woman is leaning back, eyes closed. Neither is looking at us. The maid's eyes are on the woman's hair.

I look up Degas in a book. His theory of color. As an example he speaks of hair.

A Sam Francis Painting: "Untitled (Mother and Daughter)"

for Andy Levy

(1)

He has it both ways with
this title, begins by
untitling it then

(for his painting of two
red rectangles that
appear

to be standing up
near each other) he gives
the parenthetical bond,

Mother and Daughter. They're on
two
pieces of paper, joined

by the frame. Altogether
33 by 24 inches, so not
monumental

if we want to speak of
literal
size.

(2)

If you were going to portray
yourself and your father
as two identical shapes of
any color, what would you choose?

My father answers,
grey squares. An hour later he adds

his father's
would have gold glitter
and his would not.

(3)

I ask my mother what she'd choose
for her mother and herself.
She can't decide.

Two weeks later
she still can't.

The sons I've asked
about their fathers
have all answered the same day.

Three weeks later she says
blue ovals.

"Both of us
are cool and calm, and blue

is my favorite color. Ovals

because women have round things
and I like
round things. I think of men

as squares, their square shoulders.
The Sam Francis painting looks to me
like a father and son."

(4)

Red paint. The brush dipped
into red paint. The red

brush

strokes.

Of course the
piece

actually up on the
wall

has a different
presence and hue

than how it looks
in the catalog. In the

reproduction you can't
see any of the

strokes, it's as if
you're too far away and you wouldn't even see

that the rectangles each have their
own

piece of paper
unless you looked

longer
than it takes to peel an orange.

(Degas' complaint, that almost no one
walking by a painting looks

longer than that.)

(5)

Speaking
of his work, Sam Francis says, "The space
at the center of these paintings

is reserved
for you."

(6)

I ask a lawyer, Ted. He says royal
blue cylinders. He explains that his father
liked blue

and he and his father
love to eat. And once Ted dreamed
that he and his father

were in a car together

and strapped
to the top of the car
were two gigantic hoagie sandwiches.

(7)

Andy, my younger brother, says
he sees himself and our father
as blue squares. "I'd rather be a square

than a circle
because it seems more masculine.
And I like blue.

I don't want to be weak.
And I don't want to be too showy.
A square for Dad, too, because he's quiet

and strong."

I ask
why a square seems quiet.

He says, "Blue
is the quiet."

(8)

Sam Francis painted the two red rectangles
when he was about 57. Younger,

he'd often paint simple forms, but by this time
he usually painted big, complex works overlaid

with splashes, spatters and drips. In a movie
shown continuously at the museum he

stands above a piece of paper and, with
watercolors, makes a large dark grey rectangle

with diminishing grey rectangles inside it. The rectangles
shimmer. He lifts

his brush
and shakes grey across the rectangles, changing

the order he'd created into something less balanced, more
sense of chance and space.

Every other painting in this small show
has such spots or streaks or dribbles.

When he painted these red rectangles he didn't throw,
drip or flick paint at them

or across them. The two or three little drops of red
outside the rectangles

seem accidental (though he probably could have
wiped them off), mistakes

left visible.

(9)

Jerry, a large, stocky man, about 65, excellent
at repairs, has told me that years ago
he built an airplane from a kit then flew it. He glances
at the painting in the catalog, says

he sees himself and his father as "a single peanut
shape, with black and grey swirls. And he's
the black
and I'm the grey."

"Why a peanut?"

"We're nonconformists, so we're
weird shapes. We both think
in black-and-white
type situations. We go
our own ways, yet we're exactly
the same."

"But if you try to think," I reply, "of two
identical shapes
for yourself and your father,
would you be two peanuts?"

"No, we'd still be one peanut."

"Do you have any special associations
with peanuts?"

"No. Don't even
like 'em that much. It was just
the first thing
that came into my mind."

(10)

Sam Francis says, "Red contains
every color, even red."

Assuming
that is true, this red

mother and daughter
contain all colors

while sharing the exact same shade.

(11)

Sam Francis' father
was a professor of mathematics, which may
or may not

have something to do
with his choice of these two
rectangles

to stand both for so much that is
untitled

as well as for a
mother
and daughter.

His mother
was a pianist.

(12)

I ask Leah, the waitress at the restaurant
where I'm a regular. She says she and her mother
don't get along. Her mother's legally blind
and wears almost black sunglasses. Leah says

she had begun wearing similar sunglasses
and that wearing them, and feeling like her mother,
is comforting. She says, "I need to think
about your question."

A week later, she says, "I see my mother
and myself
as interconnected rings. Not free.
I haven't come up

with a color, although yellow
occurs to me. Thanks. I liked
thinking about this. Would you give me
another one?"

PHILIP GUSTON

As a boy Philip came home. He was 10
or 11. As a boy he came home

and found his father
had hanged himself.

He was the first to find his father.
Philip was the youngest of seven.

His father hung himself
from a rope thrown over a rafter.

He found his father. And he began to draw
cartoons. He shut

himself in, at home, in a large closet with its one
light bulb, and he'd draw.

Draw draw draw draw draw draw draw.
Repeated, it almost begins to sound

like a crow's call, or sound like the opposite of
snow, nothing white falling from the sky but,

instead, the pencil lead and what hand
makes appear

out of a hidden place
or a place that wasn't there before, that only he

could bring to life.

GUSTONKY

A typo, of course. But
I like the word. Philip Guston's

"real" last name was Goldstein. The other
day I heard, for the first

time, someone say aloud
"nomenclature." It sounded like

a ring of keys, heavy keys. The man
who said it pronounced it

slowly. Nomenclature
sounds like a creature, six

thin legs and that dull black body
with two antennae sticking up and trembling

above red eyes. It doesn't bite, moves
very slowly. Guston's late paintings do bite, slow

you down. Where were you going any
way. Philip

painted himself with his head barely
above

a flood, or a floor, painted himself
as a head, detached from a body, often mouthless, hard to

say much without a mouth, can't say a name, can't
ask for keys and hands are

elsewhere anyway so aren't there to hold them
or anything. One big open eye.

Philip Guston's "Head and Bottle"

A large
self-portrait profile

as if he were a profligate
who opened the gates to

alcohol, as if the word
were also alcohole or alcohell. One-
eyed de-

capitated head

discolored blue and

red, leaned over an inch
away from a green bottle that points its

mouth
away from him. He

has no mouth. He needs a
shave. His absurd head, noseless, has one ear

but the universe looks noiseless. The bottle is not half

as distorted as the head, the painting disgusting-
ly, disGustonly, as if he would

cast off his cartoon head, leave it to look but not drink,

as if painting could disinherit the mouth.

THE SCULPTOR DAVID SMITH (1906-1965)

David Smith, when he was 3 or 4, got tied to a
tree. His mother

was a teacher, his father an unsuccessful
inventor working for the phone company.

One of them tied him up
because he kept running away

to his grandmother's house. That
wet day he sculpted a lion out of mud.

A Sculpture for the Painters
Don Cole and Joan Wortis

A row of eleven commas, each
balanced
on the brown earth
with no pedestal and standing
straight, each 16 feet tall, sculpted

in granite, encountered
in a clearing in the woods
unexpectedly, punctuation
seeming out of place, no words
between the commas only

this view of the woods
between them. As if Noguchi
had been commissioned
by Levy
to create this

gathering.
Each weighs a ton and offers
smoothed curves. Stable and massive, they
provide rounded places for these red and
green and orange and black and yellow

birds

who sing
now
without punctuation

RELEASED

The birdbath is fluted, and I lie under our big tree and look over at it, thinking of temples I've seen in The World Book. The birds always stay on the ground, pecking. The bowl on top is half full of rain and old leaves. I'm sure that as soon as I go away the birds will walk around the rim of the bowl, like senators in togas, in twos and threes, talking among themselves and pausing to look into the water, or to step in to bathe.

rain in potholes sipped by sea gulls

Clean Monday (Feb. 25, 1984, Meligalas, Greece)

for the Zambaras family

First day of Lent, the day
kites are flown. 9 a.m. I open my shutters &
feeling the wind, look at the blue for kites.

None, but the old widow
across the dirt road
has just released

her chickens.

IF THERE

If there were a poem
made of only one letter

let it be the V
growing behind this white swan

in the blue black water

Birds change places the bare tree branches.

Bird Flights

Birds'

flights

    the opposite of

             paved roads

the opposite of nails
  just
      sunk in

      or hammered long ago

the opposite of regrets

LIGHT, MIND, MOOD, SHADE

BETRAYAL

as if you were flat, a
tray, to be a tray, to be
heaped unexpectedly
with hurt

and how the hurt remains, as if
the tray doesn't ever
get tilted, is carried level and
nothing spills off

SAYING

I'd trust you
as far
as I could throw you. The first person
who said that
must've wanted to pick up the
deceiver

and throw him or her
much further
than possible. And, realizing that, the deceived

came up with words
that pick up the desire to throw
and the reality of how far we can

throw the actual weight of a
deceiver.

The Pressures

The pressures and distances
between any

one
person
pressured

and
another
distant

account
for
these

gouged
beings

Giacomettied
here

with

there

pressing
in

everywhere

FROM CHILDHOOD

In the living room, sunshine through the windows and glass door. The room bright and long. The grown-ups are in the dining room, I can hear their voices but not the words. I imagine the living room splitting off from the house, lifting and floating into space and darkness but I'm safe, can look out into the black and the bright room is still around me. The room slowly glides past stars.

Dad's friend walks in, comes over and rubs my hair. It doesn't feel good.

"What do you want to be when you grow up?"

I can tell he doesn't care. Suddenly I know I'll die before I reach ten.

"A fireman," I lie, so he'll go away.

THE NEEDLE'S HOLE

Why wasn't that hole
called the mouth?

Thread

would be breath
and words.

Or, if the hole is
an eye, it sees
the need
to bring something

and something

together

for the first time, or
to mend
a union.

The hole, then, sees
with as
single a purpose
as a believer.

The Holy Feast

We've got the word
sip, and then the word

siphon. Let's talk about fleas, then,
the small, wingless

insects of the order Siphonaptera.
The adults of both sexes

eat only blood. Their sons and daughters
emerge from eggs to eat the adult flea's

shit, as well as other organic
stuff. Fleas possess strong legs to leap

as if scattered by God
to partake of all breathing beverages.

ANGST

for Philip Rowland

No, not Ang St.,
nothing that cheery
or streetlighty or trafficked. Angst,
sounds like the proverbial

drop of water from the
faucet lengthening
then separating
so it will dive down the drain

alone. Or like a perversion
of the gerund, ill
cousin to ingst. Or leaving behind
angriest by cutting out

three letters to get straight
to the point of anxiety without
the detour
of anger. Many possible angles,

some no longer than an angstrom,
some quite long and eel-like,
anguiliform angst, sometimes living
in holes, almost always predatory.

SPITE

blame honed
and thrust

Anguish

Sounds like something squashed, squished,
stepped on, lost.

An guish
rather than a guish, as if right off

you began wrong.

EQUAL AND UNEQUAL PARTS

into the cold and dark
with a thought as big
as a football and no
where
to kick it

* * *

This overcast morning sight
is equal parts
light, mind, mood, shade. I
can sometimes
tell them
apart.

* * *

as if in counting
up to five

I got side-tracked
at one

* * *

parts of the day
like a building under construction
in a child's drawing

DESPAIR

As if there were two of them, a
pair, a pair of
whatever they are

pulling us and pulling us down,
as if one held

each foot
or each hand.

At least it's not trepair
like a horrible contradiction,
three yet two

as if the third, there
and not there, would tear
and rend, as the other two

clutch.

Or, as if des-
pair means no pair, all
alone, no one near, no one

far, with whom to share how one
became pared
to zilch.

longing: a wish to reach

awash with that wish

WRONG NUMBER

They hear your voice first.
They wanted someone else.
So did you. It's a little like
love gone wrong, but much faster.

KOKEDERA (MOSS GARDEN IN KYOTO)

the Moss Garden gardener in Kyoto
33 years ago lifted a slender stick
about 20 feet long
to dislodge from the maple tree

one
fallen autumn leaf
held between two
still attached

DOGS NAMED BINGO

Emily Dickinson and N

Emily Dickinson: ". . . to N's I had an
especial aversion, as they
always seemed
unfinished M's."

A world of the
unfinished
next to the finished. A
world, for

her, alive and
emotional, full of
seeming, all the way
down

to where a letter is never
fulfilled
no matter where
it appears.

I Read Poetry at the Dentist's

My dental hygienist tells me
I have to stop reading now. Then she
points at the poetry book I put face-down
on my lap again. She says that while the dentist
had been drilling my tooth she
read one of the blurbs on the back of the book.

"I just LOVE
to read," she says, "maybe
I'll get that book. What's it about?"
I say it's a book of excellent poetry. "Oh,
I haven't read any poetry
on a voluntary basis."

Poem for Phil

Where'd I put my sentence? My head filled and
emptied with
your poems, this year, your poems, this year.
I am better off for that.

Row row row your boat
gently – when I sang that

as a child

I didn't understand the importance of
gently.

Is this the poem called "Poem for Phil"?

Words bob up and down, down this
page, merrily. "So you're a poet, are you," she asked.
"What do you write about?" He wrote about

her question. The poem
floated downstream, the way
a bingo game is gone
after the numbers have been called and

there was a winner at the other table.
The other poem yelled BINGO
while this poem misplaced its

sentences.
"I write poems about dogs

named BINGO," he writes

hours
after she'd asked.

MY LAST READING

for David Miller

My last reading was in a narrow alley downtown and was billed as an "11:00 p.m. to 1:15 a.m. Sampling of Levy." Those who attended were instructed to choose one leg to stand upon. They were allowed to lean against the alley walls, though the grime discouraged the more pampered. My favorite panhandlers circulated freely through the small crowd, the only ones permitted to use both legs. It is more difficult to say no to a beggar, I'm told, if you are standing on one leg in a dark alley. (I read by flashlight, but the audience was in the dark, literally and figuratively.) The panhandlers reported they would have done very well indeed if the crowd had been larger than only my wife and eleven children.

KEATS, ALLY, AND I

I read Ally, 8, the first line of Keats'
"On the Grasshopper and Cricket":

"The poetry of earth is never dead."

"Of course," she
says, "poetry

is never dead."

Surprised, I say
excitedly, "Good for you!"

I am holding the Keats book, looking
at her, am about

to read the next line when she adds,

"It was never
even alive

in the first place."

TED BERRIGAN LOVED THE COLOR ORANGE

Abandon no orange, all ye who enter
the Berrigan Gates

Orange hem of morning and evening
orange hence of illogic

The orange gun shoots orange
ping-pong balls

The orange wave
Orange Crush

POETS IN THE FOURTH OF JULY PARADE

They felt they had to enter. Everyone else did.
Tapdancers, politicians, car dealers, veterans.

An illiterate man yells THANK YOU
as the poets pass.

He thinks they're more veterans. Each poet
in sandwich boards with a poem on both sides.

The man assumes the poems are lists of battlegrounds.
"I wonder what war they

fought in," he says to the stranger
next to him, in her low-cut turquoise. "The poets?" she asks.

He isn't listening, having lowered his eyes
to read the couplet of her breasts, ponder the

punctuation of two nipples. Yet he knows
she said something. "They're," he stammers,

"they're, um, all ages. I mean, they must
not've

all
fought in the same war."

Tribute to an Unknown Poet

In childhood a choice was made
by reciting a poem some unknown genius

gave us
that begins eeny meeny, and ends

the uncertainty. No other poem
gets accompanied

by one of your fingers
pointing at this, then at that, one

sound at a time, delight
in not knowing what you'll get

until you point at it out of words.

Oblivion, Tyrants, Crumbs

Today I typed "oblivision"
for oblivion. Not wanting to obliterate
that typo, I started writing this poem. In one
version I typed "tryant" for how the mistake

took me for its subject. A typo in a poem
about typos. And a self-portrait as an ant, trying
to carry the crumb of an error and erring
at that, an errant.

Poem by My Dream

First of all, let me say it's a relief to have this chance to talk to
    you.
Otherwise I feel as if I am constantly getting on
and off a bus named John Levy; it starts, stops, sometimes runs
    a red

and when I'm on I'm only another passenger and when I'm off
I'm left behind. I yell obscenities at the driver when the bus
pulls away even though the driver sees me running for it. The
    John Levy

driving the John Levy bus sees me and can obviously
lip read. Usually he can't help letting a little smile deface
any attachment I had for him in the first place. But now I

am steering. This is a whale. Don't worry, reader, you're no
    Jonah
because now we're on a glass-bottomed boat looking down
quite a way through aquamarine water at the whale circling
    below.

The whale of our emotions and lust is calm and quite gorgeous
in its enormity, restlessness and actual flesh. The old couple
    near the railing
throw their camera overboard and we watch the black camera
    sink

slowly toward the whale, land atop its back, and then tumble off
into the unknown blue. The old man whispers to his wife
he dreamed of her breasts last night and that's when we all see
    John Levy

reflected in the dark mirror eyes of the school of dreamy
brilliant yellow, red and blue, and orange fish
blocking our view of our whale. But that Levy is so small in
    those

bulging fish eyes it's impossible to know if he is smiling.
I can tell you a few things, though. If this were his poem
the lines would be considerably shorter and he would've said
    something

about whether the breasts the old man saw in his dream were
his wife's when she was in her twenties, or her thirties, or her
    forties, etc.
Awake, he runs the John Levy bus according to schedule. And
    yes,

the old man's old wife smiled
when her beloved spoke softly to her of her body
as they both rocked on the ocean.

The Blessing of the Poems

Once again hundreds of poets are lined up, in groupings they call stanzas, outside the Cathedral of St. John the Divine in New York City, waiting their turn at a Blessing of the Poems service. One young poet is singing through a megaphone in some language no one present knows (though an anonymous source claims it is a combination of Estonian, Pig Latin and baby talk in Russian). The literature professor selling ear plugs is making a small fortune.

That poet in the bright purple shirt, the one who is ripping his poems up and taping together the fragments, looks familiar to Mr. Obulaski Locatelli, the legendary reporter who has covered these blessings for the last 75 years. However, Mr. Locatelli, now 101 years old, cannot recall the poet's name and, uncharacteristically, is speaking to the TV cameras glumly rather than with his usual elated shouts.

There is an honor code. No poem should be blessed more than once. The cheaters, who bring the same poems year after year, admit that their luck got worse after they violated the honor code; they swear on a stack of Pablo Neruda books that beginning next year they'll deliver completely new poems.

READING POETRY AT 4:30 A.M.

"God doesn't evaporate,
God isn't water."

I love those lines
by Tomaz Salamun. They're

his poem's
first two lines. I'd been

thirsty
for something like that

though I'd been reading poems
rather than a prayer book.

His words could be
part of a prayer. Or the whole thing.

Then I look again, see
he wrote "Gold," not "God."

His poem is about history, capitalism, himself, others, and more.
I hadn't been thinking about God before I started his poem

and as far as I can tell
he wasn't thinking about God while writing it.

QUESTION MARKS, STARS, ARROWS

(BEGINNING

(Beginning a parenthetical statement (which
we have (and which we enter and
now enter deeper (if

parenthetical statements have
depths (they could have shallows (or
a single shallow (and a shallow is

usually a horizontal flatness whereas the
single parenthesis
is a vertical curve

(and yet how often do we stop to
look at
one (Piet Mondrian

said curves are too emotional (he banished them
from his paintings) Oh upright curve (you give
rather than hold back (Oh

lovely line seldom seen for yourself but rather
only as beginning or end, birth or
final moment of digression (digression from what, though? (does life

itself digress
from what was before and what (or what un-
what) will

arrive
after our conclusion

LOTS OF TIMES

little time to do little
no tree would think

* * *

hard not to personify the leaves
up in their trees thrown all around
by hard winds

* * *

memories of loved ones
exact enough to re-
enter and know
which way is east

* * *

My great grandfather, Rabbi Herman
Simon, ordained in Vilna, had eight
small congregations in St. Paul, Minnesota.

My mother remembers that
at his funeral one of his friends, another
rabbi, repeatedly stood up to show his watch to

the audience and the speaker in order
to make that person sit and give
the next a chance.

* * *

she says, on the way to my cousin's
burial, her mother's
ashes
                    are in her basement

* * *

very blue water bright
fallen leaves

float
inside their tree's reflection

* * *

unless asked to
who would look
under a butterfly in
flight
for a butterfly shadow

* * *

where clouds shift where

      * * *

memory of childhood home –
your bedroom, say, the view from the
window

back then

when the future whenned out
so differently from now

      * * *

over 23 years ago I was sitting on the floor
in a public building reading Maritain's
Creative Intuition in Art and Poetry
when a woman opened the door and
as I looked up I fell in love

      * * *

"Well, that's just a
thousand times
better

than anything that
happened to me
yesterday."

* * *

in my dream someone asked
if the Greeks here fish

and a Greek replied, "Everybody fish"

* * *

"We were so

fortunate

that butterfly sat on his
shoulder," Werner Herzog says

about that 18-second part of
his movie, Aguirre, The Wrath of God

right

near the end.

* * *

this clear
form from that
shiny faucet hangs
a moment in a shapely

way

* * *

no
awk-

ward-
ly

falling

snowf-
lake

HAN WU TI (156-87 B.C.)

The two lovers in the
courtyard in autumn

are no longer, as the
leaves move around them,

making love

& Han Wu Ti
explains this, saying

The rustling of the
silk is discontinued

Five Dollars in Tucson, 2007

Middle-aged
panhandler

sitting on the sidewalk
as I approach, no one else
nearby:

"Hey, with
five dollars I

could get laid

cuz

all she wants

in return
is

a bite

to REALLY

eat."

Vacant Lot Where Empress Once Stood

In Tucson today, on the bus, I passed a
razed X-rated club, the lot
just dirt now

behind a chain-link fence. All the erections
over the years, pointing and pointless,
in a place named Empress. As if

any She who has a body we want could rule us
forever, pull us around by the news of a
face, and breasts, and all the rest, the dreamed-of

reduced to dirt behind a fence, the chain-link
like fish-net stockings made of wire, as if air itself
rises like a woman's legs. Open all night. Just like the

dirt is now, the waiting dirt, the thoughtless, un-
nippled, omnipotent dirt
that waits, deep, under every thing we put up.

Eight

Your older brother, nine, is ready
to kick you, to send you back
to zero. Your younger brother, seven,
has always pointed at you.

Unlike one, you're not reduced, not
compressed between zero and two.
Three looks like your echo.
When you lie down, to rest,

you resemble your mother, infinity,
yet also look
like zero facing a mirror.
August F. Mobius found you a wife.

VOICE IN ANOTHER STATE

I want to mention a name I saw on a door:
Larry Dredge. I'm sure he

won't read this, so few people dip into poems
to gather anything, to dredge

any shallow or depth, so I'm not worried
he'll be offended when I say

What a name! A man I knew a year ago
has a stepfather whose first name

is Voice. Son of Voice. Boy, the son
couldn't fend for himself. What he did

got him
sent to prison, with Voice

in another state
and never writing.

WRITING IN USED POETRY BOOKS

I'm used to the
marginal
accolades or interpretations, question marks, stars, arrows,
exclamation points, underlined
words and phrases, the references to
other poets (such as the cursive and lovely

                                                    Blake

written to the right, carefully, of a
particularly beautiful line that doesn't
remind me of Blake), but
why

did the last owner of this poetry book I've bought
write, on the back
inside cover, in

three

lines

the following fact

The plural
of fez
is fi

which lines, I confess, I enjoy
more than any of the poems in the book, none of
which

mention

a fez
or any fi

(though it turns out the dictionary says
it is fezzes, not fi)

INSTEAD OF

for Arthur Statman

About 24 years ago the Greek boy
I was teaching English wrote, in a composition, of a

"lined tree avenue" and ever since then I've
seen it, the row of leafless trees on either side of a wide street,

each tree's intricate, etching-like lines and whorls. I imagine the
avenue empty of cars, empty of people, so that trees

are what matter most, lined
trees.

       * * *

light whys is what Arthur said
instead of
white lies

now the dark whys are likewise
coined

       * * *

In the psychiatrist's report it says the man
used angel dusk. Let us all use it.

The typist meant angel dust (PCP, a member of the
family of dissociative anesthetics) but with this typo

associated the illegal drug with one of the most wide
spread lovely states we can enter.

* * *

Improv Avenue: Improv, unproved, improvise

improve eyes
ears and

make what hasn't
gone before

and does now

new

as it turns the
corner

and progresses onto
Adios   Ave nue

Philip Guston's "Pyramid and Shoe" (1977)

Guston painted a pyramid and, near it, on the red
red land (that seems depressed
by the pyramid's weight) a grey work boot also monu-
mental. How to fully

explain that? Twin memorials? Though the shoe would rot
under a sun. Under the massive stones
the dead monarch's mummified body. You've
booked a flight to Egypt and find this gigantic shoe

next to the pyramid you'd come to see. No fellow tourists
today. But if the man
stepped into this painting, the man whose foot fit
this shoe, the pyramid would rise just a bit

above his ankle. The mummified body, then, would be
smaller than his last toe in the
titanic shoe, the little toe his mother told him
goes "wee wee wee" all the way home.

PAIN

is fifty percent
in. It's not father,

pa, added to in. If it were, the word
would partner with pa-

out, his absence. You could choose
between them or

have both in one
sentence. Drain, bane, stain, complain,

wane, pain
rhymes

with so much. Rhymes
are little songs – will sing us

a bit away
from pain's rejection

of what it can't reach. Pain has no
mascot, no Grim Reaper or Sandman, so you

don't find cartoons about Pain as its own
character, as some one or some thing distinct

from the pained
one. Pain dis-

dains who we were
without it.

PIG IN FIRST PERSON

Look, at least the U.S. Navy put me under.
There I was, a pig, anesthetized. In the advanced
trauma treatment program each corpsman
got one of us. So I'm on the floor and this teacher
shoots me in the face twice with a 9-millimeter pistol and the boy

gets all bloody picking me up, cries
as he cleans my face, manages to get one of the bullets
out of my jaw. My teeth busted and he
removes scraps of teeth and tongue from my
mouth. I want to scream, am all scream, but can't make noise

except for my breath. My legs twitch. He bandages my face. The
    teacher
shoots me in the belly with an AK-47. Then shoots me five more
    times
with the AK-47. The boy talks to me, says
he knows I can hear him, knows I want to die. He says
he won't let me. He plugs me up, has my whole body

wrapped up. He gives me morphine (the morphine
something like Heaven) and it's hour eleven now and only
one other pig is alive. The teacher blasts me with a shotgun. I
    can't see,
shotgun pellets through my eyes, my eyes this boy
can't help. Another blast shreds my neck and my back. The boy

gets me to hour thirteen. I'm the last pig alive.
All the other soldiers praise my boy. The teacher
pours lighter fluid on my bandages and lights me. The kid
puts out my fire. I make it
to hour fifteen. I wanted to live

for that boy. He cries. He tells me, You're
my pig, man, you're
MY pig, Oh
holy Hell you're my living
thing, man, you're braver than

I am, you're . . . And then I leave
that Hell. He
leaves it too, goes out to war.

INSIDE ITS SOUND

In Chinese

put the character "autumn" on top of
"heart" to make the character

"sorrow." Wu Wenying, in the 13th Century, begins a poem
by asking what sorrow is made of.

"Autumn on the heart of a man who travels," he writes
of being far from home.

CAMPAIGNS

Imagine voting once every four years not only
to elect a President but also

to add a few new words to what, and how, we
think. Who'd campaign for them? I'd wear those

campaign buttons, bringing to mind the
title of Gertrude Stein's book, Tender Buttons. Oh, to

treat words tenderly, try not
to forget how much they bestow

their largesse and
largeness, and their lovely lovely part

in governing
our thoughts.

My Paris Garret (1976)

for Michael Levy

my neighbor
also has a view

of the water
thumb-tacked up

* * *

the woman
across the wide
street

dark-haired
and beautiful
almost never

appears
on the small
balcony

outside her
curtained windows

* * *

small grocery store
on the corner

where the owner
either

172

has quite a
memory loss or

simply would rather
not acknowledge

I've entered his place
more than a hundred times

in the last six months, his
usually

empty
place

        * * *

taking the downstairs
neighbor's young son

to the Louvre, then
returning him to his

grateful mother who
insists I stay for a late

lunch and takes out
of the fridge a lump of meat covered

in white lard, says
it's rabbit

        * * *

no elevator, seven flights
as they're called in English

* * *

thin walls

African neighbors
wonderfully
polite and quiet

once when I
locked myself out
and the landlord was gone

I knocked at their door:
the African I barely
knew

when he understood I wanted to
walk the thin ledge
to my unlocked window

may have saved my life

by not even giving me a choice:
he opened his window, stepped out
and made it over

* * *

the walk to the
Seine

just
before dawn

and all
the other times

probably at least two hundred
versions of the poem about the Seine, each

keeping the phrase
diamond juggler

* * *

the same grey as
these buildings

winging
between them

lands
in the trees

Tongues & Tongs

Tongues and tongs. In English the sounds
are kin. And in German, too, die Zungen (the tongues),
die Zangen (the tongs). The tongues move words

out of silence
into air
as sound

waves

that float
us

but tongs pinch, and carry, and what
they put down
stays as down as a stone. The tongues, the tongs,

die Zungen, die Zangen, swim side
by side through this poem to reach
the bottom

where they separate and swim
disparately.

"The Cancellation of My Mind's Map"

I love that title. I closed the magazine
without reading the poem. I love that title because it suggests
our minds are worlds, so many capitals and tributaries,
coasts, islands and depths – discovered, named, visited,
inhabited or abandoned. Finally
I was ready to read the poem, opened the magazine.
I was wrong. The title is "The Constellation of My Mind's Map."
The poem is by Hwang Ji-Woo, a Korean. It's complex,
though not long. I can tell you this:
the poem is about traveling across a desert, with at least one
other person, understanding that we follow steps
"from which no one will be excused" as
"you and I are walking toward the distant blue sky"
and are led
by "the constellation of our minds' map."

THE DAY OF THE WORD

for Guy Birchard and Anne Heeney

What day
isn't?

Though we may forget.

Why not have a day each year to
celebrate language, a holiday

observed as we speak and write, as we
read and think. Any day would do. Today, say,

"as we speak," as the saying goes.

As the saying goes we go, word
by word, into our lives, our times of

understanding, and misunderstanding, our
blah blah, and those words we try hard to mean.

One day a year to praise language, to care
fully for these gifts

that come to us weathered and rich.

THE N IN HYMN

for Arthur Statman

The n in hymn
is at one with
hym, as if in silent devotion

to the h, y, and m. A scholar says hymn's n
has been silent since
1530. N's silence at the end

of hymn like the nanosecond
after a hymn is sung and we keep thinking
with the hymn rather than away from it and back

to what it is
we can't
praise.

I wish to be akin
to that n – absorbed in, and by, a
hymn, inside its sound, not wanting

or needing
to announce any
separation.

BONES AND DREAMS

ONE VERSION OF IMMORTALITY

Allyson, 7, says – as we stand
in sand at a playground – she'll live
to a hundred. Then, in
Heaven, she'll go backwards:

ninety-nine, ninety-eight, all the way
back
until
she's inside Mom again.

And then
she'll come out

and go back up
to a hundred. Back-and-forth,
forever. I ask
if God

will be in Heaven.
No.

Where will
God be?
Nobody

knows that, she answers.

Words Written in Salt

My son's homework:
learn how to spell 10 words. His teacher
suggests he write them in salt. We pour

the white
onto a metal pan. His finger
pushes aside the

white, touches into
shape
and becoming.

We stare down at these words
framed by the pan. We kneel above them
on the kitchen floor, silent.

A Drive with My Mother in 1958

My mother used to tell me (when I was in
my teens) I pronounced "picture" and "pitcher"

too much alike. My mother
a perfect pitcher of grammar,

of advice, of love, tried to picture
her son in a world where, at the very

least, he would speak
properly. As a father myself, now,

I appreciate how thankless the task.
Once she and I were in the station wagon

alone (usually I wasn't alone with her)
when I was seven. I don't know

where we were headed as we drove (no other
traffic) past the enormous graveyard

with the radio on my favorite song: "It was a one-eyed,
one-horned, flyin' purple people eater. . ."

We were rounding the curve along the
grassy cemetery. I saw no one in there,

but imagined a grown-up man, a stranger, just over the
low hill, walking slowly to a grave – to be alone

with the person buried there. Slow, thoughtful
steps, past many gravestones. And I saw my mother and me,

as if from above, as we drove by, unseen and unheard,
in our long car with our rolled-down windows

listening to the wind and a song that made us both
happy on that empty black road with its dotted white line.

Allyson, Poet-in-Residence

my four-year-old daughter
said of the moth beating
at our window
"It is made of bones and dreams."

NAT'S DRAWINGS

The creatures have all
sorts of shapes for heads, only sometimes
arms, always
eyes, often smiles. Each
being differs

from others near it. Some float, some almost
stand on a thing like ground. He points
to one, tells me it is invisible but "I just
made him visible

for you."

When Mom tells me stories about when she was a girl I can't picture her as a little girl. But then she tells me that once in her school yard her best friend began to yell at her DIRTY JEW! DIRTY JEW! For the first time I can see her as a child. And I am standing next to her, facing the girl screaming at us.

EVOLUTION

During dinner my six-year-old daughter says
she doesn't believe any of her

relatives, no matter how
far back, were monkeys.

My son, nine, says he thinks we are
related to monkeys and declares

he wants to be a Quaker
because they're

against war.

Nowhere, With God

Joking, as I often do with my four-year-old, I am
putting her to bed and say, "I've met you
somewhere

but I can't remember where."

"At home and with God," she replies.

"Do you believe in God?"

"Yes."

"Where does God live?"

"Nowhere," she says right away.

"Is God comfortable there?"

"Yes."

FIREWORKS ON NEW YEAR'S EVE

I lift my daughter
on top of my shoulders. The fireworks are off

in the distance, all over
the city lights and horizon. Small,

bright, right after midnight she
blows her tinseled paper trumpet

where we stand as the sparks appear and glorious
fall, write in the dark, make us

the readers

turning their pages, the happy
first chapter of two thousand and five.

Allyson's Threat

At seven she tells me
I've got to

stop

writing poems about her.
I say I can't.

"O-
kay,

if you
don't

I'll stop

saying fantastic things."

Poem for My Mother

Typo: dizzing. Without the y, does the word seem more dis-
orienting than dizzy but equally off-balance? Like
almost being struck by lightning? My mother
doesn't like my poems about words. But here, inside

this poem, I want to tell her I can't quite choose
what to say when I'm in the interior of a poem, it's
words in here, its words, that appear as
noise and more, like creatures, roosters, say, a dawn

or any time the words make their call. It
dawned on me, as the saying goes. Poetry
as a calling. A bit different than calling
on the phone. Last night I called my mother, told her

that last week, two days after I turned 55, I was alone
in my car
ten feet away from a tall eucalyptus when the tree
exploded, split in half by lightning, the sound a shock

before the tree crashed east, instead of
west, so I lived. A birthday gift from the
weather, my life, odd 55 with both fives like
equal halves of that tree. I didn't say that, of course, simply

told her how the tree exploded deafeningly
as I slowly drove through the parking lot listening to
NPR. If I'd been going faster I would've died. She told me
to write a poem about that. I said I'd

tried, but couldn't because I can't
write much of a poem if I know before I'm in it
what I want to say. "But," I promised, "I'll
try again."

Death

When you're dead, my seven-
year-old daughter explained,

one of the first things you do
is get lessons

on how to be invisible
so you can come back

as a ghost. And then
it's not

so different from being
alive.

I didn't get her words
verbatim, nor did I say

But you may find out, my
love, how being alive

you also get lessons
on what it is like to be invisible.

Notes

P. 15: The quote from Robert Lax is from personal correspondence with the author.

P. 27: The final line of the poem is a quote from Kenward Elmslie's poem "Motor Disturbance," which appears in *Routine Disruptions: Selected Poems and Lyrics* (Coffee House Press, 1998).

P. 28: The lines of Ted Berrigan's are from "Sonnet XXXVII," a poem which appears in several of his books, including *The Collected Poems of Ted Berrigan* (University of California Press, 2005).

P. 29: The Alice Notley quotation is from her Introduction to *The Collected Poems of Ted Berrigan*.

P. 35: The phrase of Yang Lian's is from his poem "Dismal Summer" and is translated by Brian Holton. "Dismal Summer" appears in *Where the Sea Stands Still: New Poems* (Bloodaxe Books, 1999).

P. 51: The phrase of Yang Lian's is from the poem "Metaphor,'" is translated by Brian Holton and appears in *Where the Sea Stands Still: New Poems*.

P. 56: The line of Louis Zukofsky's is from section 19 of his book *Anew*; the poem is in *ALL: the collected short poems 1923 - 1964* (Norton, 1971).

P. 146: The Tomaz Salamun poem cited is "The Trap" in his book *Feast* (Harcourt Brace International, 2000) and is translated by Christopher Merrill and Marko Jakse.

P. 177: "The Constellation of My Mind's Map," by Hwang Ji-Woo, translated by Won-Chung Kim and Christopher Merrill, appeared in the Spring/Summer 2005 issue of *Circumference: Poetry in Translation* (New York).

John Levy lives in Tucson, Arizona. He is a lawyer and works as a public defender. His book of poems, *Among the Consonants*, was published by The Elizabeth Press in 1980. His journal about living in a Greek village, *We Don't Kill Snakes Where We Come From: Two Years in a Greek Village*, was published in 1994 by Querencia Press. Four chapbooks of his poetry have been published by tel-let. He is married to Leslie Buchanan, a painter, and they have two children, Nat and Ally.